CW00959994

Vegan Cookbook for Beginners

Insanely Delicious and Nutritious Vegan Recipes for Health & Weight Loss

By <u>Karen Greenvang</u>

Copyright ©Karen Greenvang 2016

www.HolisticWellnessBooks.com

All cooking is an experiment in a sense, and many people come to the same or similar recipe over time. All recipes in this book have been derived from author's personal experience. Should any

TABLE OF CONTENTS

Introduction

As with all lifestyle choices, there are many different reasons as to why someone may choose to become vegan. Veganism is more than just a diet, it is a way of life and this little list will provide a little glimpse of the benefits:

Guilt-free Living

A vegan or plant-based diet involves no consumption of animal or animal by-products, or use of animal products (such as fur and leather). For those who are conscious about where their food and clothing originates from and how it became the final product, a vegan lifestyle sheds off a lot of that guilt.

Lower Risk of Developing Heart Disease

Plant based diets have been scientifically proved to lower your risk of developing heart disease, due to the lack and low intake of saturated fats and processed foods.

Greener for the Planet

Meat production is the largest contributor to world methane emissions due to the sheer volume of cattle that are passed through the system. Methane is a much more potent gas compared to carbon dioxide and thus by following a plant-based diet, your methane footprint is lowered. Rainforest land is often also converted to cattle grazing areas or soy bean plantations for cattle feed. This means that less deforestation will be taking place on your behalf by leaving animal products off your plate.

Chapter 1

Dangers of Consuming Animal By-Products

So what's the beef with dairy? Why should you be leaving eggs off your plate from a health standpoint?

Modern day commercial farming sees animals as produce, numbers on a spreadsheet and not real lives. This means that chemical inputs such as growth hormones and antibiotics are often given to dairy cows and hens, in order to prevent them from falling ill or to bulk up their muscle and milk producing capabilities.

The issue here is that the effects of animal hormones and chemical antibiotics on humans in the long term is still unknown. The chemicals used to increase the milk production of a dairy cow may be dangerous to a human. What's more is that these chemicals and hormones then enter our bodies and we have no way of monitoring their effects.

In general, the less chemicals within your body, the healthier you're going to be, so why add those additional hormones and antibiotics into a perfectly working system?

Animal by-products are also high in bacteria and can cause serious cases of salmonella (food poisoning) if a contaminated or 'gone off' product is consumed. What's more is that many people are finding that they're intolerant to lactose, an unsurprising fact considering that any animal naturally shouldn't be consuming milk after the lactation stage, especially not the milk of another animal. For those who grew up with dairy, the body can tolerate the lactose due to the built up colonies of lactase, the enzyme used to digest milk and dairy products.

However, some people lack these enzymes and therefore cannot digest the dairy product.

Recipe Measurements

I love keeping ingredient measurements as simple as possible- this is why I stick to tablespoons, teaspoons and cups.

The cup measurement I use is the American cup measurement. I also use it for dry ingredients. If you are new to it, let me help you:

If you don't have American Cup measures, just use a metric or imperial liquid measuring jug and fill your jug with your ingredient to the corresponding level. Here's how to go about it:

1 American Cup= 250ml= 8 fl.oz

For example:

If a recipe calls for 1 cup of almonds, simply place your almonds into your measuring jug until it reaches the 250 ml/8oz mark.

I know that different countries use different measurements and I wanted to make things simple for you.

Translations (US-UK English)

Eggplant   =   Aubergine

Zucchini   =   Courgette

Cilantro   =   Coriander

Garbanzo Beans   =   Chickpeas

Navy Beans- =   Haricot Beans

Aragula   =   Rocket

Broth =   Stock

Chapter 2:

Insanely Good and Healthy Vegan Recipes

PART I:

BREAKFAST RECIPES

Avocado smash on toast

Serves: 1

Avocados are a known superfood and with good reason! These green gems are packed with vitamin E, an essential nutrient for clear, healthy and glowing skin. They're perfect for breakfast as they are both creamy and filling, setting you up perfectly for the day ahead.

Avocados can be tricky in terms of judging how ripe they are and when to slice into them. You can gage whether your avocados are ready for use by gently squeezing one with your hand. If the avocado squashes slightly, it is ready to eat. Do not use hard avocados for this recipe as you will end up with a bitter tasting topping!

This recipe works brilliantly on any kind of toast, although if you couple this idea with a homemade sourdough bread, you'll find a new level of appreciation.

Ingredients:

- ½ avocado

- Coconut or vegetable spread

- Sundried tomato or olives (optional)

- Marmite or vegemite or vegan spread of your choice

- (optional)

- Seasoning (sea salt, ground black pepper)

Method:

1. Toast your bread in the grill or toaster.

2. Slice the avocado in half using a bread knife and scoop

3. out ¼ of the flesh into a bowl.

4. Mash the avocado using a fork and season.

5. Spread a layer of coconut spread, marmite or vegemite onto your toast (optional).

6. Spoon the avocado smash onto the toast and top with sundried tomatoes and olives (optional).

Easy Vegan Flax Seed Mix

Serves: 2-4

Great option for breakfast on the go! Easy, tasty and nutritious. Give yourself the energy you deserve!

Ingredients:

- 2 avocados, peeled, pitted and chopped
- 1 cup almond milk or coconut milk
- 1 tablespoon ground flax seeds (chia could work great
- here, too)
- ½ cup soy sprouts
- Olive oil and Himalayan salt to taste

Instructions:

Blend and enjoy!

Tofu Scramble

Serves: 1-2

A quick and easy alternative to traditional scrambled eggs, tofu scramble is a great way to get a portion of protein into your body for breakfast. This recipe can be jazzed up by adding your favorite combination of herbs, olives, sundried tomatoes, nuts and spices. You can serve tofu scramble individually or on toast.

Ingredients:

- 1-2 cups firm tofu

- Vegetable oil

- 1 clove of garlic

- Sundried tomato or olives (optional)

- Mushrooms and baby spinach (optional)

- Seasoning (sea salt, ground black pepper, turmeric, basil)

- Organic non GMO soy milk or almond/coconut milk (you choose!)

Method:

1. Lightly heat up your frying pan with a drizzle of vegetable oil and fry your garlic with any additional spices (turmeric provides a bright yellow coloring for aesthetic appeal).

2. Remove tofu from packaging, rinse under cold water and place between a few sheets of kitchen roll.

3. Gently squeeze the tofu to remove additional water.

4. Throw tofu into the frying pan and break into pieces with a spatula.

5. Add any additional veggies such as mushrooms or baby spinach leaves.

6. Season with your desired herbs and toppings.

7. Fry on a medium heat for around 5 – 8 minutes, allowing the tofu to brown slightly on the edges.

8. Serve alone or on toast.

Tasty Quinoa Bowl

Servings: 2

Quinoa is full of natural protein and will keep you full till lunch. This is a fantastic vegan, gluten-free porridge with anti-inflammatory properties.

Ingredients:

- 1 cup uncooked quinoa, rinse well

- 1 ½ cups water

- ½ teaspoon ground cinnamon

- ½ teaspoon nutmeg

- Stevia or maple syrup to sweeten (yum!)

- Pinch of Himalayan salt

- Optional- almonds and other nuts

- Optional- dried fruit or banana slices to taste

Instructions:

1. In a saucepan, combine the quinoa, water, cinnamon + other spices of your choice and salt.

2. Bring to a boil.

3. Then, turn down the heat, cover, and simmer for about 8 minutes.

4. Keep stirring well until cooked.

5. When cooked, remove from the heat.

6. Cool down by pouring down some almond or coconut milk.

7. Enjoy!

This recipe is great with some barley grass powder.

To learn how I use vegan superfood in my smoothies and other recipes, get my free, complimentary eBook: "Vegan Superfood Smoothies".

Download Link:

www.bitly.com/karenfreegift

Vegan Paleo-Friendly Porridge

Servings: 1-2

This recipe offers a highly energizing mix of seeds, spices and vitamin C. No excuses- don't skip breakfast.

Ingredients:

- ¼ cup chopped walnuts

- 2 tablespoons pumpkin seeds

- 1 tablespoon raw chia seeds (optional)

- 1 teaspoon ground cinnamon

- 1 teaspoon nutmeg

- 1 cup almond milk or coconut milk

- 1 tablespoon of melted coconut oil

- Juice of 1 grapefruit or orange (I love to blend orange juice with coconut milk- try it!)

Instructions:

1. Combine your ingredients in a cereal bowl and pour over some coconut milk.

2. Stir well and serve. Yum!

Amaranth Coconut Porridge

Servings: 2

Amaranth is a great source of iron and is also gluten-free. Great for a balanced vegan diet.

Ingredients:

- 2 cups water
- 1 cup amaranth
- 1 cup coconut milk

Instructions:

1. Add amaranth to boiling water.
2. Reduce heat and simmer on medium heat for 15- 20 minutes until amaranth is cooked.
3. Remove from heat and add the coconut milk.
4. Add some maple syrup to sweeten if you wish.
5. Enjoy!

Banana Bites

Serves: 2

This little recipe takes around 20 minutes to prepare, but the effort is worth the outcome! Bananas are the perfect 'start your day' fruit, packed with potassium and providing a steady release of sugar and energy. Due to the natural sugars present in the bananas, using unsweetened apple juice and apple sauce is the best way to avoid an overly sweet end product. This recipe makes a dozen bites. This recipe is also beautiful with a handful of frozen blueberries added to the mixture.

Ingredients:

- 4 overripe bananas (brown)

- ½ tablespoon of baking powder

- 2 cups of ground oats

- ½ cup of applesauce

- ½ cup of apple juice (not from concentrate)

- 1 teaspoon of ground cinnamon

- 1 ½ tablespoons of flax seed

- ½ tablespoon of apple cider-vinegar

- ½ tablespoon of vanilla extract (natural)

- ½ teaspoon of baking soda

Method:

1. Pre-heat oven to 350 degrees Fahrenheit. (175 Celsius)

2. Line your muffin tray with liners.

3. Add all dry ingredients into a large bowl.

4. Puree the bananas in the processor until smooth.

5. Add the wet ingredients to the processor and mix again.

6. Pour into bowl with dry ingredients.

7. Mix gently.

8. Pour mix into liners, ¾ full.

9. Bake until golden brown (20 minutes approx.)

Savory Pancakes

Serves: 1

These savory chickpea pancakes are a high protein, sugar-free alternative to the conventional breakfast treat. They can be topped with avocado, salad, fried peppers, wilted spinach and any other veggies. These pancakes will keep you going through till the afternoon and are the perfect flavorful kick starter for your day.

Ingredients:

- Spring onions (chopped finely)
- ¼ cup of Red Bell Peppers (chopped finely)
- 1 clove of garlic
- ½ cup of Besan (chickpea) flour
- ¼ teaspoon of sea salt (finely ground)
- Water
- Toppings: Guacamole, salsa, hummus etc.

Method:

1. Lightly heat frying pan and prepare veggies.

2. Whisk up the flour, seasoning and baking powder in a small bowl.

3. Add in ½ cup of water and mix until smooth, creating air

4. bubbles.

5. Stir the chopped vegetables through.

6. Drizzle oil onto pan and pour batter to make one pancake.

7. Cook on each side for around 5 minutes and flip when

8. browned.

9. Serve hot with toppings.

Granola Swirl

Serves: 1

This super quick and easy recipe can be made up in one glass, within 5 minutes! It is also packed with calcium, protein and antioxidants. This combination can be adapted with your favorite fruits and nuts, providing a different range of flavors and nutrients every time. If you have spare time on your hands, you can also stew apple, sugar and water to provide a deeper layer of taste and satisfaction. Served in a glass to display the layers, this stunning breakfast is one you won't forget!

Ingredients:

- ½ handful of blueberries
- ½ cup granola
- Dairy free yoghurt
- Agave nectar
- 2 pitted dates

Method:

1. Layer a glass with a spoonful of dairy free yoghurt.

2. Add a spoonful of granola.

3. Add a layer of chopped dates and blueberries.

4. Repeat the layering process and finish with the yoghurt.

5. Swirl on the agave nectar for the finishing touch of

6. sweetness.

PART II:

LUNCH RECIPES

Mediterranean Penne

Serves: 1-2

This vibrant lunchtime dish is the perfect partner for a packed lunch! It takes just under 20 minutes to prepare and can be made up in batches that could be stored in a fridge or even frozen for times when you don't have the chance to cook up something fresh.

Ingredients:

- Penne pasta (about half cup per person)

- 1 bell pepper (or ½ of two color variations)

- ½ cup olives (pitted)

- 1 clove of garlic

- ¼ cup of extra virgin olive oil

- ½ cup of roasted almonds (roughly chopped)

- Seasoning (basil, salt pepper)

- 1 red onion (finely chopped)

- Handful of fresh thyme

- 1 tbsp. yeast flakes

Method:

1. Boil and cook the penne as instructed on packaging.

2. Heat up a frying pan with oil.

3. Fry the garlic and onion for 5 minutes.

4. Chop and prepare the veggies.

5. Cook veggies in the pan with the garlic and onion, until slightly charred.

6. Once pasta is cooked, drain using a sieve and rinse to remove any starch.

7. Season veggies and serve up the pasta, top with veggies and a drizzle of olive oil.

8. Chop up the thyme leaves and sprinkle on top.

9. Add some yeast flakes to your dish for additional flavor

10. (optional).

Vegan Sandwich Feast

Serves: 1-2

Layer up this beauty for a filling and wholesome afternoon meal and serve with potato chips for an additional crunch factor. You can combine the ingredients with any dip or sauce, providing you with numerous options if you have to take your lunch out and about with you. If you're enjoying this lunch at home, you can lightly toast your bread for added flavor.

Ingredients:

- 2 pieces of wholemeal bread (give fruit bread a try if you have a sweet tooth!)

- Hummus

- 1 Roma tomato

- 1 clove of Garlic

- 1 cup of Basil (fresh leaves)

- 2 tablespoons of lemon juice

- 2 tablespoons of olive oil

- ¼ cup of hemp seeds

- 6 sundried tomato slices

- 2 tablespoons water

- Avocado

- Red pepper flakes (or chilli flakes)

- Seasoning (salt and pepper)

Method:

1. Layer your hummus onto one slice of bread and sprinkle the pepper or chilli flakes.

2. Slice up the avocado and add to the slice of bread.

3. Top with slices of tomato.

4. Mix up the rest of the ingredients in a food processor to make the pesto.

5. Spread pesto onto the other slice of bread and sprinkle with salt and pepper.

6. Combine both slices for the perfect lunchtime feast!

Nuts About Salad

Serves: 2

Who says that vegan salads are pure leaves and rabbit food? You can enhance the nutritional value of any green salad by throwing in some nuts and seeds. This recipe tosses the conventional salad rules out of the window – Prepare your taste buds!

Ingredients:

- ¼ cup Rocket Lettuce

- ¼ cup Iceberg Lettuce

- ¼ cup Baby Spinach Leaves

- 1 Sweet bell pepper, sliced

- ¼ cup Cos Lettuce

- 1 orange (peeled and sliced into small chunks)

- Trail mix

- Olive oil

- Some Basil leaves (fresh)

- Lemon Juice (1/2 lemon)

- Grated carrot

- ¼ cup sultanas

- Seasoning (ground black pepper)

- Hummus (optional)

Method:

1. Prepare the dressing by combining olive oil, fresh basil leaves and lemon juice.

2. Wash all of the salad ingredients thoroughly and leave to drain.

3. Once the leaves have drained, mix them together in a large bowl, creating the bed of the salad.

4. Season with ground black pepper.

5. Add in thin slices of the sweet bell pepper and grated carrot.

6. Mix in the orange slices (apple slices may also be used) and sultanas.

7. Pour the dressing and toss the salad.

8. Sprinkle the trail mix over the salad before serving.

9. Serve with hummus (optional).

Stuffed Cucumber

Serves: 1-2

This neat recipe involves the preparation of a "mock tuna" salad, served and presented in slices of cucumber. As the almonds require soaking for optimum softness (6-8 hours), be sure to plan this meal the night before.

Ingredients:

- 1 clove garlic (mashed)

- 1 cup of almonds (raw and soaked)

- 2 stalks of celery (finely chopped)

- 2 spring onions (finely chopped)

- 3 tablespoons of vegan mayonnaise

- 1 teaspoon of mustard (Dijon)

- Seasoning (black pepper, sea salt, lemon juice)

- 1 large cucumber (chopped into 1cm thick rounds)

Method:

1. Grind up the almonds in a food processor to create the

2. 'tuna' flakes and add to mixing bowl.

3. Throw in all of the filling ingredients and mix together.

4. Use a teaspoon to scoop out the innards of the cucumber, creating a small hole in the center of each round.

5. Season the cucumber and scoop the filling into the hole.

6. Serve as a platter or try out the mixture in a wrap, pitta or with salad leaves for future variation.

Black Bean Quinoa Salad

Serves: 2-3

This high protein salad is made up of beans and grains rather than pure salad leaves. This dish is gluten-free and can also be made with other grains or cous cous, depending on your preference. You may even decide to mix things up on the next level and combine different grains for added taste and texture.

Ingredients:

- ½ cup of pine nuts

- 1 ½ cups of quinoa (or other preferred grains)

- 2 Roma tomatoes (finely diced and peeled)

- 1 cucumber (English, finely diced)

- ½ red onion (finely chopped)

- ¼ cup extra virgin olive oil

- Can of black beans

- ½ cup of fresh parsley (finely chopped)

- 2 teaspoons lemon zest (grated finely)

- 3 tablespoons of lemon juice

Method:

1. Pre-heat oven to 400 degrees Fahrenheit. (200 Celsius)

2. Prepare quinoa or grains as instructed.

3. Lay out a baking sheet onto the baking tray.

4. Sprinkle pine nuts onto tray and brown them in the oven for a couple of minutes.

5. Rinse out the canned black beans and add to mixing bowl.

6. When browned, throw the nuts into the mixing bowl and add in all of the other ingredients.

7. Make up the dressing and stir through.

8. This dish can be served as a hot or cold salad.

Raw Green Smoothie

Serves: 1

This smoothie is a real life saver when you are pressed for time. You can also have it with some quinoa or make it thicker and

use it as a dip to have with some raw veggies.

Ingredients:

- 1 Apple, green is best (take out the core)

- 4 Celery stalks

- 1 Cup baby Spinach

- 1 ripe Avocado

- 1 bunch cilantro (no stems)

- 3 cups spring water

- ½ fresh-squeezed lemon

- ¼ tsp cayenne pepper (optional)

- 1 cup Coconut milk

- Himalayan salt to taste

Method:

Blend and enjoy!

Cool Vegan Veggie Soup

Serves:

Whenever you feel like you need more energy- resort to raw foods!

Ingredients:

- 1 avocado

- 1 zucchini

- 3 celery stalks

- 2 handfuls baby spinach

- ½ cup both parsley and cilantro

- ½ cup raw almonds

- Pinch of sea salt

- Pinch of cayenne

- 1 ½ cups of spring water (or 2 depending on how thick you want it)

- Juice of 1 lime

Method:

1. Cut any large ingredients into smaller pieces if necessary and put everything into a blender and mix well.

2. Enjoy!

OPTIONAL:

It tastes amazing with natural, vegan-friendly coconut milk or coconut cream.

PART III:

DINNER RECIPES

PB Tofu Slices With A Sauce

Serves: 3-4

Peanut butter and tofu combined, yes that's right, heaven can exist within the kitchen! Load up on your protein with this rich, spicy and satisfying Asian cuisine inspired meal.

Ingredients:

- 3-4 cups of firm tofu

- 3 garlic cloves (finely chopped)

- 1 knob of ginger (peeled and finely grated)

- 1 tablespoon of peanut oil

- 1 spring onion (sliced finely for garnishing)

- 3 tablespoons of soy sauce (reduced salt)

- 2 tablespoons of smooth peanut butter (reduced salt and sugar)

- 3 tablespoons of rice vinegar

- 1 tablespoon of agave nectar

- 2 tablespoons of water

Method:

1. Drain out the tofu and squeeze between sheets of kitchen towel to remove excess water.

2. Make the sauce by whisking the vinegar, soy sauce, peanut butter, water and agave nectar.

3. Prepare the spring onion, garlic and ginger.

4. Heat up the wok and add oil.

5. Cook the ginger and garlic until fragrant then remove and set aside.

6. Add the tofu pieces and cook on a medium heat, flipping them over and allowing them to brown on either side (this should take 5-8 minutes).

7. Once the tofu slices have browned, pour in the sauce and cook until thickening occurs.

8. Add the garlic and ginger along with the spring onions and garnish.

9. Season and adjust the sauce flavor if necessary.

Squash Risotto

Serves: 1

Creamy, vibrant and wholesome – This recipe takes a classic dinner dish (risotto) and combines it with fresh basil, summer squash and peas. It's the perfect meal for those uplifting summer evenings.

Ingredients:

- 1 onion (finely chopped)

- 2 tablespoons of olive oil

- 2 cloves of garlic

- 4 cups of vegetable stock

- 1 cup of Arborio rice

- ¼ cup of white wine

- ½ cup of frozen peas (thawed)

- ¼ cup of fresh basil leaves

- Ground black pepper

- 1 tablespoon of vegan margarine or a dash of dairy free

milk

Method:

1. Prepare the squash by washing and slicing into crescents

2. (1 ½ inches thick), set aside.

3. Heat up a large saucepan with olive oil and add the garlic and onions.

4. Sauté for 5 minutes on a medium heat.

5. Stir the rice into the pan and cook for a further 2 minutes.

6. Add in the white wine and stir gently until the liquid is absorbed.

7. Add the stock into the pan one ladle at a time.

8. Stir frequently and allow the liquid to be absorbed before adding more.

9. After 15 minutes, add in the peas and squash.

10. Repeat the process of adding water, stirring and cooking for another 5 minutes until the creamy risotto texture is visible.

11. Remove the pan from the stove and add the margarine

and fresh basil leaves.

12. Stir gently.

13. Season with pepper, garnish with basil leaves and add a
    little lemon juice for an added zing!

Vegan Spaghetti Squash

Serves: 2

Fantastic combination of taste and health!

Ingredients:

- 2 medium to large spaghetti squash

- 12 diced roma tomatoes

- 1 diced onion

- 4 cloves minced garlic

- 1.5 tablespoons evoo (olive oil)

- Sea salt to taste

- Pinch of stevia

- ¼ cup basil chopped

- 5 or 6 sundried tomatoes

Method:

1. Cut squash in half. Remove the seeds.

2. Place face down in pan with 2 cups of water.

3. Bake in oven at 300 degrees for an hour or until tender enough to pull out spaghetti strings.

4. While it is baking, fry up the onion and garlic in the evoo until onion is clear.

5. Put in the tomatoes (roma and sundried).

6. Turn heat to low and cook for 8 minutes.

7. Add half of the basil, salt and stevia (only a tad).

8. Take half of this mixture and blend in your blender.

9. After, put it back in with the other mixture.

10. Loosen the "noodles" in the squash.

11. Spoon sauce over the squash and sprinkle remaining basil.

12. Top with almond "cheese."

Almond "Cheese"

- 2/3 c. raw almonds

- 1 large clove garlic

- ¼ tsp sea salt

Simply put all ingredients in food processor or blender and mix until fine.

Lentil Curry

Serves: 1-2

This recipe is easy to prepare with any vegetables that you have in the house. It is also a brilliant dish that freezes well, allowing you to stock up for those days when cooking is not on the cards. Vegan, healthy and a convenience dish? Let's dig in!

Ingredients:

- 1 cup of white, button mushrooms (roughly chopped)

- 1 onion (large, chopped finely)

- 2 potatoes (white or red, cubed)

- 6 cloves of minced garlic

- 1 knob of fresh ginger (peeled and grated)

- 2 teaspoons of coriander

- 1 tablespoon of masala (garam)

- 1 can of chopped tomatoes

- 2 teaspoons of red chili powder

- 2 cups of spinach (chopped and washed)

- 3 cups of water or vegetable stock

- 1 cup of red lentils (washed and soaked)

- Fresh coriander leaves (garnishing)

- 1 teaspoon of sea salt

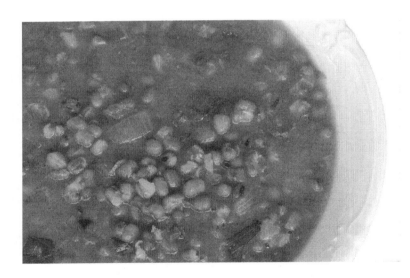

Method:

1. Heat a tablespoon of oil in the saucepan and cook the
   onions, mushrooms and salt on a medium heat until
   the mushrooms are golden brown and the onions
   translucent.

2. Add potatoes and cook until edges turn translucent.

3. Add the garlic, ginger and spices into the middle of the pan and cook for 30 seconds until the garlic becomes fragrant.

4. Stir in the spices, add the tomatoes, lentils and spinach.

5. Stir well to combine the ingredients and pour in 3 cups of stock/water.

6. Turn the heat up and bring to a boil.

7. Then reduce the intensity and simmer for approximately 45 minutes, allowing the lentils and potatoes to cook though.

8. Add any additional seasoning for flavor and garnish with

9. coriander leaves (fresh).

Tacos De Papa

Serves: 1-2

Potato tacos! A filling and deeply satisfying dish which will tide you over for hours. This Spanish meal is bright in color and super easy to prepare.

Ingredients:

- 4 tablespoons of olive oil

- 2 red potatoes (peeled and cubed)

- 2 chilli peppers (Poblano)

- 2 cloves of garlic (chopped)

- 1 onion (chopped)

- 2 stalks of celery (chopped)

- 1 ear of white corn (stripped of all kernels)

- 1 lime

- Fresh corn tortilla wraps

- Seasoning (salt and pepper)

- Avocado (diced)

- Fresh coriander leaves (chopped)

Method:

1. Pre-heat the oven to 450 degrees (Fahrenheit).-230 Celsius

2. Heat 3 tablespoons of olive oil in a frying pan with the potatoes.

3. Fry until crisp and brown on the outside.

4. Using gloves, slice the chillies in half, remove seeds.

5. Line a baking dish with oil and place the peppers onto the dish.

6. Roast in oven for approximately 10 minutes.

7. Chop the chilies and set aside.

8. Once the potatoes are cooked, place them on a plate lined with kitchen paper.

9. Cook the remainder of the ingredients in oil on the stove

10. for five minutes and squeeze in the lime juice.

11. Heat the tortillas for 5 minutes.

12. Layer the tacos with potato, chillies, vegetables and garnish with coriander.

Super Quick Stir Fry

Serves: 2-3

Making a stir fry takes little time, preparation skill or extensive pre-shopping. You can whip up a stir fry using the ingredients in your cupboards and this recipe will provide a baseline to which you can add and take as you please.

Ingredients:

- 3 cups noodles
- Sesame oil
- Handful of cashews
- ¼ cup of sesame seeds
- 1 cup tofu (marinated in soy sauce for 1 hour, cubed)
- Broccoli
- 2 carrots
- Spinach

- Bean sprouts

- 1 clove garlic

- 1 knob ginger

- Chinese 5 spice

- round black pepper

- Snow peas

- 1 tbsp. soy sauce

- Corn flour (1 tablespoon)

- Shallots (1/2 cup)

- Pak choi

Method:

1. Prepare the veggies, wash thoroughly and chop up into smaller pieces for faster cooking.

2. Prepare noodles as instructed.

3. Heat the wok with sesame oil and fry the garlic, onions and ginger until fragrant.

4. Add in the tofu and cook for a further 5 minutes.

5. Stir in the vegetables and fry for 5 minutes.

6. Add in the soy sauce, a tablespoon of water and seasoning.

7. Use the cornflour to thicken the sauce if necessary.

8. Throw in the cashews and garnish with sesame seeds.

PART IV:

SNACKS AND TREATS

Nutty Date Rolls

Serves: 2

Being vegan certainly doesn't rule off dessert from the menu.
In fact, it makes the dessert menu even more appetizing in
many ways! This simple recipe is not only free of added
sugar, but it is raw vegan dessert – No oven needed!

Ingredients:

- 1 cup almonds or cashews (raw)
- 1 tablespoon of orange juice
- Desiccated coconut flakes
- ¾ cup of pitted dates
- Trail mix
- 1 tablespoon of almond meal
- 1 tablespoon of cinnamon

Method:

1. Place the nuts, dates, trail mix, almond meal and cinnamon into the food processor.

2. Blend using a grinding blade (add in the orange juice when the blades stick).

3. Sprinkle the coconut over an area of the worktop.

4. Shape the mixture into rolls or balls, in the palm of your hand.

5. Roll the balls in the coconut.

6. Refrigerate in an airtight container.

Chocolate Mousse Treat

Serves: 2-3

Re-creating the texture of a conventional, diary mousse may sound like a difficult proposition, however the wonders of silken tofu take up the challenge perfectly. These indulgent little desserts can be made and stored in miniature pots and frozen for future sweet tooth cravings.

Ingredients:

- 1 cup dark chocolate (dairy free)
- ½ cup maple syrup
- 2 cups silken tofu
- Zest of 1 lime
- 1 tablespoon of dark rum
- Sea salt
- 1 tablespoon vanilla extract

Method:

1. Drain the tofu and blitz it in the food processor until smooth.

2. Melt the chocolate.

3. Add the chocolate and remaining ingredients into the food processor.

4. Mix until a mousse forms.

5. Refrigerate for at least 30 minutes before serving.

Apple And Peanut Butter Sarnies

Serves: 1

A sandwich for dessert you say? What's going on? This clever little recipe uses fresh apple slices as bread' and peanut butter, nuts, choc chips and sultanas as a sweet filling. Healthy and naughty – the perfect balance for a vegan dessert!

Ingredients:

- Fresh apple (sliced into rings)

- Peanut butter (no added salt or sugar)

- Sultanas or raisins

- Ground nuts

- Dairy free chocolate chips (check out the baking aisle for dark choc chips)

- 1 tsp. Cinnamon

Method:

1. Core the apples and slice into rings (less than 1cm thick, for ease of cutting into).

2. Slather one slice of apple with peanut butter and top with raisins, choc chips and nuts.

3. Sprinkle cinnamon on the top and place another ring above to complete the sandwich.

4. Place on a baking tray lined with baking parchment and bake for 10 minutes at 350 degrees Fahrenheit. (175 Celsius)

Lemon & Berry Vegan Cheesecake

Another raw vegan dessert, this cheesecake is chock full of natural enzymes, a guilt-free and healthier adaptation of the traditional dairy dessert. Any assortment of berries can be used for this cheesecake, you could go for raspberries or blueberries, or even go all out and create a 'forest fruits' cheesecake using a range of different berries. The contrasting zest of the lemon and the sweetness of the berries make this dessert a truly indulging experience.

Ingredients:

- 1 cup of pitted dates

- 2 cups of almonds (raw)

- ¾ cup of lemon juice (freshly squeezed)

- 3 cups of cashews (soaked for at least 60 minutes)

- ¾ cup of agave nectar

- ¾ cup of liquid coconut oil

- 1 teaspoon of vanilla extract

- ½ cup of water

- ½ teaspoon of sea salt

- 3 cups of frozen berries

- ½ cup of dates or agave nectar (for berry sauce)

Method:

1. Place almonds and dates into the food processor and blend to create the cheesecake base.

2. Press the mixture into the base of a spring form pan.

3. Blend the cashews, lemon juice, agave, coconut oil, water, vanilla extract and sea salt in the food processor to create the cream cheese.

4. Blend until smooth.

5. Pour cheese mixture onto the crust and tap the pan on the work surface to remove any air bubbles trapped in the mix.

6. Place cheesecake into the freezer for 3-4 hours, allowing

7. firming to occur.

8. Transfer to fridge and remove when ready to eat (please note that coconut oil will melt at a warm temperature,

so don't keep the cheesecake out of the fridge for long periods).

9. Make the berry sauce by blending the berries and dates (or agave) until smooth, slather on top of cake when serving and decorate the cake with a few whole berries.

Banana Bread

Serves: 5-7

This baking classic is not solely a dessert for the lunchboxes of children. It can be a beautiful addition to any afternoon tea, cholesterol free and dairy free. If you make this loaf with gluten free flour, then it will also be coeliac friendly. The key to the perfect loaf is to pounce on blackened bananas, when they are over ripe, but just before they become pure sugary masses. Doing so will allow for a reduction in the sugar needed within the recipe.

Ingredients:

- 1/2 cup brown sugar (adjust according to banana ripeness)

- 3 cups plain flour (or self-raising)

- 3 heaped teaspoons of baking powder (if using self-raising flour, only use 2)

- 3 teaspoons of mixed spice or cinnamon

- 3 large overripe bananas (mashed)

- ½ cup dried fruit, nuts and chocolate chips (dairy free,

- optional)

- ½ cup coconut or vegetable oil

Method:

1. Pre-heat the oven to 392 degrees Fahrenheit. (200 Celsius)

2. Mash bananas using a fork and mix in the sugar and oil until they are well combined.

3. Mix in the flour, cinnamon and baking powder using a

4. wooden spatula.

5. Add any additional ingredients such as dried fruit, nuts, chocolate chips and mix through well.

6. Spoon mixture in an oiled baking loaf tin for twenty minutes.

7. Check on the loaf and cover with foil if browning has occurred.

8. Bake for a further 40 minutes (approximately).

9. Allow the loaf to cool for 20 minutes before slicing.

10. Texture will turn soft and gooey when left overnight, making it a delicious treat when its fresh out of the oven and even more so a few days later.

Chocolate Oranges

Serves: 2

Easy to make and super yummy!

Ingredients:

- 5 oranges, mandarins or clementines (peeled and
- separated)
- ½ cup dark chocolate pieces
- Sea salt

Method:

1. Line a baking tray with parchment paper.

2. Place the chocolate pieces into a small glass bowl and place over boiling water in a saucepan, medium to low heat.

3. Once the chocolate has melted, take each orange slice and dip it halfway in the chocolate, place it onto the tray, then place into the fridge to harden the chocolate.

4. Place them into a serving bowl and enjoy!

Almond And Coconut Macaroons

Serves: 2-4

Yummy and easy. Chia seed eggs are a fantastic, healthy and cruelty-free egg replacement!

Ingredients:

- 2 cups unsweetened desiccated coconut
- ½ cup almond slices
- 2 chia seed"eggs"
- ¼ cup agave nectar
- 1 tsp vanilla extract

Method:

1. Preheat oven to 350°F.
2. Line your baking tray with baking paper.
3. In a mixing bowl, whisk the agave nectar and chia "egg

4. whites".

5. Then, add the desiccated coconut, vanilla extract and almonds and mix everything together.

6. Take a soup spoon and scoop up some of the mixture and form the dough into individual macaroons, place onto the baking tray and into the oven for 12 mins.

7. When they turn golden brown, take them out of the oven, let them cool down and then serve.

Coconut Water Fruit Pops

Serves: 2

Packed with nutrients and color!

Ingredients:

- 2 kiwis (halved and sliced)

- 8 strawberries (halved)

- 16 blueberries

- 16 raspberries

- 1 ½ cups coconut water

- Popsicle molds

Method:

1. Fill the popsicle molds with an equal amount of the fruit.

2. Then fill with coconut water to the top.

3. Place the popsicle sticks on top of each, then place into the freezer and freeze for at least 5 hours or until solid.

4. Take them out of the freezer and enjoy!

ambercup coconut milk dessert

Serves: 1-2

Creamy, tasty and nutritious! Just delicious!

Ingredients:

- 1 ambercup squash (Pumpkin substitute)

- 2 cups coconut milk

- ¼ cup agave nectar

- 2 tsp ground cinnamon

- 1 chia seed "egg white" (not real egg)

- ¼ tsp nutmeg

Method:

1. Start by cutting the top off of the squash and spoon out all of the seeds inside.

2. Place the squash into a large saucepan and add with a few inches of water, but not enough to cover the squash. Place onto a plate and set aside.

3. Simmer over a medium heat for about 15 minutes until the

4. flesh inside is soft.

5. In a bowl, add the agave, coconut milk, chia egg white, cinnamon and nutmeg and stir to combine.

6. Pour the coconut mixture into the squash, use it as a bowl.

7. Eat the squash as with the coconut mixture.

8. Serve and enjoy!

Baked Apple Chips

Serves: 1-2

Easy and you can always experiment with different spices and toppings.

Ingredients:

- 3 apples
- Ground cinnamon to taste

Method:

1. Preheat oven to 220°F.

2. Line a baking tray with parchment paper and set aside.

3. Slice the apples thinly and place onto the baking tray.

4. Dust some cinnamon on top of them and place them into the oven for 1 hour.

5. Then flip the slices and cook for another hour.

6. Take them out of the oven and allow them to cool.

7.   Serve and enjoy this tasty little treat!

Creamed Spinach

Serves: 2

Fantastic way to add more spinach into your diet. Green, alkaline and vegan! Great for energy!

Ingredients:

- 2 cups baby spinach

- 2 cups coconut milk

- 1 onion (finely chopped)

- 3 crushed garlic cloves

- 2 tbsp tapioca starch

- Pinch ground nutmeg

- Pinch cayenne pepper

- 3 tbsp sunflower seed butter

- Sea salt

Method:

1. In a saucepan melt the sea butter over a medium heat.

2. Then slowly whisk in the tapioca starch and cook for 5 mins.

3. Add the garlic and onion to the saucepan and cook for another minute.

4. Then add all of the spinach and cook until softened.

5. Add in the cayenne pepper, coconut milk and nutmeg, stir everything and cook for another 5 mins.

6. Season with sea salt and serve.

Carrot And Rutabaga Mash

Serves: 2

How to fall in love with veggies...

Ingredients:

- 1 ¼ cup rutabaga (peeled and chopped)

- 1 ¼ cup carrots (peeled and chopped)

- 4 tbsp coconut oil

- 1 tbsp fresh parsley

- Sea salt

- Black pepper

Method:

1. Place the rutabaga and carrots into a large saucepan and cover with water.

2. Bring the water to a boil on medium heat and reduce to a simmer. Then cover with a lid slightly and let it simmer for 20 mins or until really soft.

3. Drain water and mash with a masher and add the coconut oil.

4. Season with the salt and pepper and sprinkle with fresh parsley to serve.

Berry Crumble

Serves: 4

Who said that you can't enjoy delicious baking goods on a vegan diet?

Ingredients:

- 4 cups fresh or frozen mixed berries

- 1 cup almond meal

- ½ cup almond butter

- 1 cup oven roasted walnuts, sunflower seeds, pistachios.

- ½ tsp ground cinnamon

Method:

1. Preheat oven to 350°F.

2. Crush the nuts using a mortar and pestle.

3. In a bowl, combine the nut mix, almond meal,

cinnamon and almond butter and combine well.

4. In a pie dish, spread half the nut mixture over the bottom of the dish, then top with the berries and finish with the rest of the nut mixture.

5. Bake for 30 minutes and serve warm with natural vegan vanilla yogurt.

Chocolate Banana Boats

Serves: 1-2

Great for quick energy or before a workout.

Ingredients:

- 2 bananas

- ½ cup dark chocolate (broken into pieces)

- 2 tbsp desiccated coconut

Method:

1. Preheat oven to 300°F.

2. Do not remove the banana skin, just slice the skin down one side of the banana.

3. Fill each banana with the chocolate pieces and desiccated coconut.

4. Roll each banana in foil and place on a baking tray.

5. Cook for 20 – 25 mins.

6. Serve hot.

Marinated Beets

Serves: 2

I love it as a quick, re-energizing snack!

Ingredients:

- 3 cups sliced beets

- 2 onions (sliced in thin rounds)

- 1 tbsp sunflower seed oil

- 2 sprigs fresh thyme

- 1 cup white wine vinegar

- ½ tsp sea salt

- 6 garlic cloves

- Pinch black pepper

- 2 x 1 quart jars

Method:

1. Preheat oven to 400°F.

2. Prepare the beets by scrubbing them of any excess dirt and remove the root and stems.

3. Line a large baking dish with foil and place the beets onto

4. there and drizzle with one tablespoon of sunflower oil.

5. Garnish them with thyme. Then seal the excess foil over

6. the beets and roast for 1 to 1 ½ hours until soft.

7. Now, remove from the oven and allow to cool. When they are warm remove the skin, then allow to cool completely.

8. Place the onions into a large bowl and cover with hot water so that they begin to tender, for 10 mins.

9. When the beets have cooled, slice them into ¼ inch rounds.

10. Once the 10 minutes has passed, start layering the onions and beets in the jars.

11. In a small mixing bowl, add the salt, cloves, pepper and vinegar, mix to combine. Then, pour half of the mixture into each jar.

12. Seal the jars then place them into the fridge for at least one day before serving.

Coffee Flavored Chocolate Mousse

Serves: 2

Excellent combination of taste and flavors... allow your senses to indulge...

Ingredients:

- ¼ cup dark chocolate chips or squares
- 1 tbsp. ground coffee beans
- 1 tbsp. vanilla extract
- ½ cup coconut milk
- ¼ cup boiling water
- 1/4 tsp mint extract

Method:

1. In a medium skillet, melt the chocolate over a low heat to prevent burning and stir frequently with a wooden spoon.

2. Add in the coconut milk and combine with the chocolate.

3. In a small bowl, mix the boiling water with the ground coffee beans.

4. Now, combine the coffee bean mixture, chocolate mixture, vanilla and mint extract.

5. Pour the mixture into 2 large dessert dishes and place into

6.   the fridge for 2 - 3 hours. To allow them to become
     firm.

7. Take them out of the fridge and enjoy!

Maple Roasted Parsnip Chips

Very simple recipe, great for beginners!

Ingredients:

- 5 cups parsnips

- ¼ cup coconut oil

- 3 tbsp. maple syrup

Method:

1. Preheat oven to 392°F.

2. Peel the parsnips, cut them into chip sizes and place them into an oven proof dish.

3. Drizzle with coconut oil generously until covered and then do the same with the maple syrup.

4. Bake in the oven for 15 minutes, until crisp.

5. Remove from the oven and turn them over to cook on

the other side for another 10 – 15 mins.

6. Remove from oven, allow to cool and then serve.

Gingerbread Cookies

Serves: 2-4

Great treat full of flavor and anti-inflammatory spices.
Health and taste combined!

Ingredients:

- 1 cup almonds

- ½ cup desiccated coconut

- ½ cup coconut milk

- 2 chia eggs

- 15 pitted dates

- 2 tbsp coconut oil

- 1 tsp allspice

- 1 tbsp cinnamon

- 1 tbsp ginger powder

Method:

1. Preheat oven to 300°F.

2. If the dates are hard, soak them in coconut milk for 15 mins.

3. Add the desiccated coconut and almonds into a food processor and process until they are finely ground. Then transfer to a bowl.

4. Now, process the dates, chia eggs, coconut milk, coconut oil and spices until smooth.

5. Stir the almond mixture into the coconut milk mixture and combine.

6. Line a baking tray with parchment paper and spread 2 tablespoons of the mixture onto it, like you would dough cookies, or you can use cookie cutters and add it to them.

7. Sprinkle the cookies with a bit more desiccated coconut and place into the oven for 15 minutes or until hard and golden brown.

8. Serve with a glass of almond milk.

Free Complimentary eBook

Smoothie Recipes

Insanely good + super healthy, 100% vegan smoothies with secret ingredients...YUM...

Visit:

www.bitly.com/karenfreegift

and secure your free copy now!

Problems with your download? Email me, I will help:
karenveganbooks@gmail.com

Conclusion

Thank you for reading!

I hope that with so many vegan-friendly recipes you will be motivated and inspired to start your journey towards meaningful veganism, vibrant health and total wellbeing.

Remember, the beauty of incorporating nutritious vegan foods into your daily diet is that you are making simple, yet sustainable changes that will work for your wellness long-term. Not to mention your spiritual wellness and taking care of the environment.

If you enjoyed my book, it would be greatly appreciated if you left a review so others can receive the same benefits you have. Your review can help other people take this important step to take care of their health and inspire them to start a new chapter in their lives.

At the same time, you can help me serve you and all my other readers even more through my next vegan-friendly recipe books that I am committed to publishing on a regular basis.

I'd be thrilled to hear from you. I would love to know your favorite recipe(s).

Don't be shy, post a comment on Amazon!

- Questions about this book? Email me at: karenveganbooks@gmail.com

Thank You for your time, Love & Light,

Until next time-

Karen Vegan Greenvang

More Vegan Books By Karen

Available in kindle and paperback in all Amazon stores

You will find more at:

www.amazon.com/author/karengreenvang

Printed in Great Britain
by Amazon